FRANCIS FRITH'S
CLITHEROE

PHOTOGRAPHIC MEMORIES

BORN AND BRED in Lancashire, **CATHERINE ROTHWELL** has been associated with local history for forty years. Daughter of a professional photographer and a Fellow of the Library Association, before retirement she was Deputy Borough Librarian of Fleetwood, and was later in charge of all reference and local history books for Lancashire Library in the Borough of Wyre. Her sixty published books reveal an in-depth knowledge of Lancashire and above all, the intrinsic spirit of a valiant shire rich in tradition. Catherine lives in Poulton-le-Fylde, and has three children and four grandchildren.

FRANCIS FRITH'S
PHOTOGRAPHIC MEMORIES

PHOTOGRAPHIC MEMORIES OF BRITAIN
CLITHEROE

CATHERINE ROTHWELL

First published in the United Kingdom in 2004 by
Frith Book Company Ltd

Hardback Limited Subscribers Edition 2004
ISBN 1-85937-810-2

Paperback Edition 2004
ISBN 1-85937-811-0

Text and Design copyright © Frith Book Company Ltd
Photographs copyright © The Francis Frith Collection

The Frith photographs and the Frith logo are reproduced under licence from Heritage Photographic Resources Ltd, the owners of the Frith archive and trademarks

All rights reserved. No photograph in this publication may be sold to a third party other than in the original form of this publication, or framed for sale to a third party. No parts of this publication may be reproduced, stored in a retrieval system, or transmitted, in any form, or by any means, electronic, mechanical, photocopying, recording or otherwise, without the prior permission of the publishers and copyright holder.

British Library Cataloguing in Publication Data

Francis Frith's Clitheroe - Photographic Memories
Catherine Rothwell

Frith Book Company Ltd
Frith's Barn, Teffont,
Salisbury, Wiltshire SP3 5QP
Tel: +44 (0) 1722 716 376
Email: info@francisfrith.co.uk
www.francisfrith.co.uk

Printed and bound in Great Britain

Front Cover: **THE CASTLE ENTRANCE** *1921* 71136

The colour-tinting is for illustrative purposes only, and is not intended to be historically accurate

Frontispiece: **MARKET PLACE** *1921* 71131

AS WITH ANY HISTORICAL DATABASE THE FRITH ARCHIVE IS CONSTANTLY BEING CORRECTED AND IMPROVED AND THE PUBLISHERS WOULD WELCOME INFORMATION ON OMISSIONS OR INACCURACIES

CONTENTS

FRANCIS FRITH: VICTORIAN PIONEER	7
CLITHEROE - AN INTRODUCTION	10
THE TOWN	15
THE HALLS	49
WHALLEY, SAWLEY AND WADDINGTON	53
THE VILLAGES	67
INDEX	87
NAMES OF SUBSCRIBERS	88
Free Mounted Print Voucher	91

FRANCIS FRITH
VICTORIAN PIONEER

FRANCIS FRITH, founder of the world-famous photographic archive, was a complex and multi-talented man. A devout Quaker and a highly successful Victorian businessman, he was philosophical by nature and pioneering in outlook.

By 1855 he had already established a wholesale grocery business in Liverpool, and sold it for the astonishing sum of £200,000, which is the equivalent today of over £15,000,000. Now a very rich man, he was able to indulge his passion for travel. As a child he had pored over travel books written by early explorers, and his fancy and imagination had been stirred by family holidays to the sublime mountain regions of Wales and Scotland. 'What lands of spirit-stirring and enriching scenes and places!' he had written. He was to return to these scenes of grandeur in later years to 'recapture the thousands of vivid and tender memories', but with a different purpose. Now in his thirties, and captivated by the new science of photography, Frith set out on a series of pioneering journeys up the Nile and to the Near East that occupied him from 1856 until 1860.

INTRIGUE AND EXPLORATION

These far-flung journeys were packed with intrigue and adventure. In his life story, written when he was sixty-three, Frith tells of being held captive by bandits, and of fighting 'an awful midnight battle to the very point of surrender with a deadly pack of hungry, wild dogs'. Wearing flowing Arab costume, Frith arrived at Akaba by camel sixty years before Lawrence of Arabia, where he encountered 'desert princes and rival sheikhs, blazing with jewel-hilted swords'.

He was the first photographer to venture beyond the sixth cataract of the Nile. Africa was still the mysterious 'Dark Continent', and Stanley and Livingstone's historic meeting was a decade into the future. The conditions for picture taking confound belief. He laboured for hours in his wicker dark-room in the sweltering heat of the desert, while the volatile chemicals fizzed dangerously in their trays. Back in London he exhibited his photographs and was 'rapturously cheered' by members of the Royal Society. His reputation as a photographer was made overnight.

VENTURE OF A LIFE-TIME

Characteristically, Frith quickly spotted the opportunity to create a new business as a specialist publisher of photographs. He lived in an era of immense and sometimes violent

change. For the poor in the early part of Victoria's reign work was exhausting and the hours long, and people had precious little free time to enjoy themselves. Most had no transport other than a cart or gig at their disposal, and rarely travelled far beyond the boundaries of their own town or village. However, by the 1870s the railways had threaded their way across the country, and Bank Holidays and half-day Saturdays had been made obligatory by Act of Parliament. All of a sudden the working man and his family were able to enjoy days out and see a little more of the world.

With typical business acumen, Francis Frith foresaw that these new tourists would enjoy having souvenirs to commemorate their days out. In 1860 he married Mary Ann Rosling and set out on a new career: his aim was to photograph every city, town and village in Britain. For the next thirty years he travelled the country by train and by pony and trap, producing fine photographs of seaside resorts and beauty spots that were keenly bought by millions of Victorians. These prints were painstakingly pasted into family albums and pored over during the dark nights of winter, rekindling precious memories of summer excursions.

THE RISE OF FRITH & CO

Frith's studio was soon supplying retail shops all over the country. To meet the demand he gathered about him a small team of photographers, and published the work of independent artist-photographers of the calibre of Roger Fenton and Francis Bedford. In order to gain some understanding of the scale of Frith's business one only has to look at the catalogue issued by Frith & Co in 1886: it runs to some 670 pages, listing not only many thousands of views of the British Isles but also many photographs of most European countries, and China, Japan, the USA and Canada - note the sample page shown on page 9 from the hand-written Frith & Co ledgers recording the pictures. By 1890 Frith had created the greatest specialist photographic publishing company in the world, with over 2,000 sales outlets - more than the combined number that Boots and WH Smith have today! The picture on the next page shows the Frith & Co display board at Ingleton in the Yorkshire Dales (left of window). Beautifully constructed with a mahogany frame and gilt inserts, it could display up to a dozen local scenes.

POSTCARD BONANZA

The ever-popular holiday postcard we know today took many years to develop. In 1870 the Post Office issued the first plain cards, with a pre-printed stamp on one face. In 1894 they allowed other publishers' cards to be sent through the mail with an attached adhesive halfpenny stamp. Demand grew rapidly, and in 1895 a new size of postcard was permitted called the court card, but there was little room for illustration. In 1899, a year after Frith's death, a new card measuring 5.5 x 3.5 inches became the standard format, but it was not until 1902 that the divided back came into being, so that the address and message could be on one face and a full-size illustration on the other. Frith & Co were in the vanguard of postcard development: Frith's sons Eustace and Cyril continued their father's monumental task, expanding the number of views offered to the public and recording more and more places in Britain, as the coasts and countryside were opened up to mass travel.

Francis Frith had died in 1898 at his villa in Cannes, his great project still growing. The archive he created continued in business for another seventy years. By 1970 it contained over a third of a million pictures showing 7,000 British towns and villages.

FRANCIS FRITH'S LEGACY

Frith's legacy to us today is of immense significance and value, for the magnificent archive of evocative photographs he created provides a unique record of change in the cities, towns and villages throughout Britain over a century and more. Frith and his fellow studio photographers revisited locations many times down the years to update their views, compiling for us an enthralling and colourful pageant of British life and character.

We are fortunate that Frith was dedicated to recording the minutiae of everyday life. For it is this sheer wealth of visual data, the painstaking chronicle of changes in dress, transport, street layouts, buildings, housing, engineering and landscape that captivates us so much today. His remarkable images offer us a powerful link with the past and with the lives of our ancestors.

THE VALUE OF THE ARCHIVE TODAY

Computers have now made it possible for Frith's many thousands of images to be accessed almost instantly. Frith's images are increasingly used as visual resources, by social historians, by researchers into genealogy and ancestry, by architects and town planners, and by teachers involved in local history projects.

In addition, the archive offers every one of us an opportunity to examine the places where we and our families have lived and worked down the years. Highly successful in Frith's own era, the archive is now, a century and more on, entering a new phase of popularity. Historians consider the Francis Frith Collection to be of prime national importance. It is the only archive of its kind remaining in private ownership. Francis Frith's archive is now housed in an historic timber barn in the beautiful village of Teffont in Wiltshire. Its founder would not recognize the archive office as it is today. In place of the many thousands of dusty boxes containing glass plate negatives and an all-pervading odour of photographic chemicals, there are now ranks of computer screens. He would be amazed to watch his images travelling round the world at unimaginable speeds through internet lines.

The archive's future is both bright and exciting. Francis Frith, with his unshakeable belief in making photographs available to the greatest number of people, would undoubtedly approve of what is being done today with his lifetime's work. His photographs depicting our shared past are now bringing pleasure and enlightenment to millions around the world a century and more after his death.

CLITHEROE
AN INTRODUCTION

CLITHEROE is an ancient market town, honour and borough in the once extensive parish of Whalley, and its history stretches back into the mists of time. Its name means 'the hill by the waters'. Saxon and Roman relics have been found, but history proper began with the ancient, feudal reign of the Lacy family, who came over with William the Conqueror.

As their share in the great prize of conquest, the Lacys claimed '60 knights' fees in Lancashire and Yorkshire'. To maintain their power, they built two castles, one at Pontefract, the other at Clitheroe. At Clitheroe justice was dispensed and moneys, taxes and tithes were demanded at stated periods. The Lordship of Pontefract and the Honour of Clitheroe was vested in the Lacys, and as power came directly from the sovereign, William I, there was no gainsaying it. It is small

DOWNHAM, *The Village 1921* 71189

wonder that for hundreds of years this extensive area was steeped in wars, battles and bloodshed. After one encounter with the Normans near Edisford Bridge, it was said that the waters of the River Ribble flowed red with blood.

Ilbert de Lacy possessed the Honour of Clitheroe, whose castle was built either in the reign of William I or in that of his son, William Rufus. It was described then as 'situated on a conical crag of rugged limestone ... A mile to the south is Pendle Hill which seems to lift its head above the clouds', an observation that holds good today. Originally the castle was a keep with a tower, surrounded by a wall and entered through an arched gateway.

Clitheroe's first charter was granted in the time of Henry de Lacy, who died in 1147. The borough was represented in Parliament from the days of Elizabeth I, when two members were called to replace Baron Clitheroe and Baron Wyresdale.

An east Lancashire shepherd on the slopes of Pendle Hill wrote:

'Oft on Pendle's side one hears
A passing sound of distant bells.
No legend old nor human wit
Can tell us whence the music swells,
Tis thought that they by Assheton brought
From Whalley's convent towers,
Still call at times the drowsy monks
To prayers at midnight hours'.

This is a sly reference to the lords of the manor taking stone and three bells from Whalley Abbey. Pendle Forest had eleven vaccaries set up by those monks for breeding cattle. Pendle Hill has been an important landmark from ancient times; beacons were fired there and in the surrounding hills - Parlick Pike, Darwen Moor, Coupe Law, and Rivington Pike - at great moments in history. 'Grand old Pendle' is indivisible from the infamous Lancashire witches' trial, and more than any other physical feature in the county it typifies Lancashire. In the neighbourhood of Pendle there are sprawling towns like Nelson, Colne, Burnley, and Padiham, where once 'King Cotton' reigned supreme.

By 1821 Clitheroe, which fell into the vast parish of Whalley, had 3213 inhabitants. Only 550 houses are listed at that date, so one may presume that there was great overcrowding. It is interesting to note that some names of the townspeople in an early directory, including the town builders and tradesmen Ashworth, Barlow, Cronshaw, Haworth and Stevenson, are family names which crop up again and again over the years. In the early 19th century there were five fixed fairs, two in May and one each in July, August and December.

There were twelve inns, which denotes a fair amount of commerce; amongst them were The Buck, The Dog and Partridge, The Calf's Head, The Cart and Horses, The Red Lion, The White Lion and The Dun Horse. Jane Silverwood's Swan Inn, still with us, came in for criticism by John Byng in 1792: 'my bedchamber was wretched with an old broken deal door through which every passenger in the house could see me in bed.' However, John Byng did praise the boiled mutton chops and a good fire. The cold wind off Pendle had aggravated his bad chest, for which he was anxious to get a 'blister', a mustard plaster. The Swan was very particular in its shoeing of horses, yet still Mr Byng complained. Such characters come with every age.

Clitheroe was noted for its torchlight processions, and the expertise of its ox-roasters was recruited by other towns. (There was an ox-roast in 1902 to celebrate the coronation of Edward VII). Notable in processions were the Clitheroe Morris teams, which were formed in 1884; the dance figures were designed in such a way that the team could continue moving with the procession. Clitheroe Borough Races (they originated on the Low Moor and ended in 1839) featured a sale of 'well-bred ponies' at The Black Bull Inn, and they are mentioned in Nicholas Assheton's diary of 380 years ago.

Clitheroe's workhouse was nicknamed 'the tramps' paradise'. In 1900, 5000 tramps passed through every year. Mr Martin, the master in the 1900s, joked: 'so often do we see some, they are as well known as the inmates!' It was all due to the Clitheroe tradition of liberal help.

The Carnegie Library was opened by John Eastham in 1905, and on the same day the library clock was set going by Mrs J T Whipp, the mayoress. Bicycles proliferated from Bensons at 14 Market Place when the cycling craze came in, and Whalley, Sawley and the Halls were besieged by sightseers.

In 1854 the Clitheroe Waterworks Company had been formed, and the first sod of Marylebone Reservoir had been cut in spring 1855 by John Eastham. It had a capacity of 500,000 gallons, and by the following year, 471 houses in the borough were receiving piped water. The 1878 Corporation Act empowered the taking over of the waterworks and gasworks companies. Within another 10 years, Alderman Garnett had cut the first sod of a second reservoir on 23 April 1887. In the 1920s, extra cables were laid to bring electricity.

CHATBURN, *The Village 1921* 71178

Some famous people have been connected with Clitheroe. The son of a well-known 18th-century vicar, James King, was educated at the Grammar school and sailed with Captain Cook. Dr Roger Bannister, the first man to run the 4-minute mile, is descended from the local Bannister family. In Pendle Heritage Centre, an oak chair dated 1623 is preserved in the Bannister room.

Complaints today are aroused by the Castle Cement factory, but most agree that Clitheroe is a healthy town - it is high, breezy and clean. In some ways it is unique. At times of high unemployment elsewhere, Clitheroe had full employment.

Walks down alleyways off the main streets can be rewarded by sudden stunning views of the countryside stretching beyond the town towards the area known once as 'Paradise' and to brooding Pendle Hill, its bulk like a basking whale, forever mysterious. Frost-edged in clear air and silhouetted against blue sky, or mist-topped, grey and forbidding, Pendle never fails to surprise and to evoke a sense of awe.

The Ribble Valley itself, designated an Area of Outstanding Natural Beauty, is on Clitheroe's doorstep, and the townspeople are as proud of this as they are of the pageants and ox roasts. Clitheroe was granted a new Royal Coat of Arms in 1952. Among Clitheroe Corporation's plate is

WHALLEY, *The Abbey 1894* 34330

a long silver mace presented in 1672. On the day of the mayor's election (yes, Clitheroe was one of the few towns with the right to retain its mayor) this is on show with a massive silver punch bowl. Traditionally, the Town Sergeant, wearing robes and a cocked hat, carries the mace; he is followed by the Head Waiter bearing the steaming punch bowl, which contains a brew made from a secret and ancient recipe. The great shout that goes up is 'Prosperation to the Corporation', a shout that has reverberated through the years since the town's first charter. Its green wax seal shows Henry de Lacy on horseback, visor down and carrying a drawn sword.

No one can deny that this is a hard act to follow, and Francis Frith's wonderful photographs help to bring the message home.

CLITHEROE PARKIN

Firth and Son of the Ideal Bakery, Clitheroe, in the early 1900's used that novelty the aeroplane to advertise "Firth's parkins are good". Their renowned RICH CLITHEROE PARKIN was made as follows:-

1 lb (450g)	oatmeal
1/2 lb (225g)	lard
1/2 lb (225g)	butter
1/4 lb (110g)	sugar
2 oz (50g)	ground ginger
1/2 lb (225g)	golden syrup

Melt lard and butter together then mix with the syrup. Add the dry ingredients mixing all thoroughly. Bake in a slow oven for 2 hours in a large, well greased tin.

Parkin was usually eaten three days old when it had softened.

There is a reference to "the famed Clitheroe parkin" in Castle Street c1960 C122018 on page 29.

CLITHEROE - THE TOWN

THE CASTLE *1899* 42902

William the Conqueror rewarded knights and mercenaries who had fought for him at the Battle of Hastings in 1066 with large tracts of land in conquered Britain. Ilbert de Lacy, a Norman knight, became one of the most powerful men in the north of England. His reward of land stretched from Clitheroe to Pontefract, fifty miles away. Henry de Lacy, Lord of the Honour of Clitheroe, granted the borough's first charter, and the town was ruled from the castle between 1147 and 1177. Courts were held in the castle. The street names ring with associated history: Castlegate, Marketgate, Wellgate. The forests of Bowland, Ribchester and Chipping were all part of the Honour of Clitheroe.

FRANCIS FRITH'S - CLITHEROE

THE CASTLE HOUSE
1899 42905

Clitheroe Castle dates back to the 12th century. Built on a grand limestone eminence, it dominates the skyline, along with the parish church of St Mary Magdalene. This castellated building, built in 1723, was used by the Steward, who lived here with his family and servants. 'Kitchen, buttery, cellar, milk house, and parlour' are listed in its inventory, but it now houses the North West Sound Archives and Clitheroe Museum.

THE CASTLE *1927* 80535

The immensely strong keep, whose history dates back to the 12th century, survived all attempts to destroy it. The last siege occurred in 1644 during the Civil War. 4000 Parliamentary troops had not been paid and lost faith in their leader, Colonel Assheton. They marched from Bowland and besieged Clitheroe Castle. Seen as a threat to Cromwell's Commonwealth, the castle was ordered to be slighted.

CLITHEROE - THE TOWN

THE CASTLE ENTRANCE *1921* 71136

This photograph shows the corner of Moor Lane and Castle Street (Moor Lane is one of the entrances into Clitheroe). The castle entrance lies behind the horse-drawn cart and the stone wall (centre); the visitor approaches up Castle Street, passing the Castle Restaurant (notice the little girl standing outside it, right). Next door is Bailey's Paragon Toilet Room, where gentlemen could get a shave and buy tobacco. A steep climb past tree-lined slopes brings one to the keep with its six acres of surrounding land, once virtually a township in itself, exempt from the jurisdiction of Clitheroe borough, a right which continued until 1895. The ancient church of St Michael within the castle walls was long recognised as the parish church of the Forest, but it was razed to the ground in one of many skirmishes.

THE CASTLE GROUNDS *1921* 71141

The grounds extend to 16½ acres. When the Normans built Clitheroe Castle they built a keep, a gatehouse and defensive walls behind the surrounding ditches. The bowling green of 1970 is now part of the castle grounds. The castle playing fields provide sports facilities, and the castle bandstand offers some grand concerts (including a recital by the baritone Frank Lord and a performance by The Tonics). Sheepdog trials have also been held here.

THE CASTLE GROUNDS *1927* 80542

The castle grounds were purchased from Lord Montagu and passed to the people of Clitheroe in 1920. Essential work on the grounds cost £15,000, which was found by fund raising. Pride of place goes to the war memorial in the Garden of Remembrance; Clitheroe men who died in the Boer War are not forgotten. The keep and the grounds are impressive, especially when they are floodlit on special occasions.

CLITHEROE - THE TOWN

THE VIEW FROM THE CASTLE *1921* 71129

This excellent view of the main route through Clitheroe was taken from the highest point on the keep. The road sweeps from the castle entrance, then goes past The Swan and Royal Hotel (the building on the right projecting into the wide pavement) and down to the market place and library. Then it climbs Church Street towards Church Brow, where the tall spire of the parish church can be seen (centre left) looking over the open country beyond.

FRANCIS FRITH'S - CLITHEROE

CLITHEROE - THE TOWN

THE VIEW FROM THE CASTLE *1895* 35712

The castle keep commands a good view of the town. Within the ten years after 1895, as many as 17 spinning and weaving mills were to appear; they were viewed with some dismay from the height of the castle, but they provided welcome employment. A complex system of roads had long radiated from the town. In 1755 the ancient trackway to Skipton was turnpiked, the first in the Clitheroe area to be transformed.

FRANCIS FRITH'S - CLITHEROE

▼ THE CASTLE ENTRANCE 1921 71135

Limestone from nearby quarries was used by the Norman soldiers who built the castle. Mussels and cockles from ancient seas, embedded in the limestone, have been found in the castle masonry. Medieval wells provided the town's water supply until the mid-19th century. The one in Parson Lane, Stocks Well, still runs. The building on the left on Castle Gate housed John Mitchell & Sons' business.

▶ MARKET PLACE
c1950 C122002

On market days earlier in the century goods were sold in the triangular area of the Market Place, and stalls extended into Castle Street; but as the market became busier, a special site had to be provided. On the left is F Dawson's shop, 'the house for quality'; next door is the Advertiser and Times, and beyond that Chapman's shoe shop.

CLITHEROE - THE TOWN

◀ **MARKET PLACE**
c1950 C122001

This photograph was taken on the same spot and at about the same time as C122002 (on page 22). On the right hand side of Castle Street is Tailor's outfitters, their windows crammed with clothing as was then the way of shop keepers; next door is the Roybeck Café. A motorised vehicle approaches, but as yet vehicular traffic is sparse - it was probably early in the day.

▶ **CHURCH STREET** *c1960*
C122021

Over 150 years ago, Church Street was the main way out of the town to Chatburn. Dates can be seen on house frontages - one drainpipe bears the date 1757. The old road wound through Pimlico, but the 1826 turnpike road was straight, passing Clitheroe Hospital, once the workhouse. Spring water in cans at 5 old pence was hawked about the streets by one enterprising native before piped water came. Thirsty navvies would appreciate that, and perhaps even John Macadam himself. He was an advisor in the construction of the road.

FRANCIS FRITH'S - CLITHEROE

▼ BRUNGERLEY BRIDGE *1921* 71139

Brungerley was long-favoured for its Good Friday and other Bank Holiday celebrations. It was the first outlet for fun following the long winter after Christmas festivities. In 1906 it was recorded that thousands came from Burnley and Padiham besides Clitheroe. Eli Tucker and his sons David and Charles of Brungerley Farm supplied boats.

▶ BRUNGERLEY BRIDGE *1894* 34346

Besides supplying rowing boats and large craft for family parties, the Tucker family offered swings, a roundabout and a tearoom by 1900. At that date bathing was allowed, and changing huts were provided - however, girls and ladies had to bathe upstream. This group of children have been posed by the bridge, and although not all have managed to keep stock still as requested by the photographer, the scene exudes 1894 Bank Holiday spirit.

CLITHEROE - THE TOWN

◄ **BRUNGERLEY BRIDGE** *1895* 35713

Brungerley Bridge is still popular today because of its proximity as a leisure area to Clitheroe town. In the 1890s it was thronged with skaters when the river froze in the severe winters of those days. My father was known as champion skater because he managed with only one leg and a crutch. Clement Houghton lost the use of his other leg at an early age, and travelling from Blackburn with a friend, he skated at Brungerley in the winter of 1895. Here, a solitary oarsman on the river and a short line of boats drawn up but not in use indicate a less busy time, perhaps early autumn; the pleasant walk alongside the river could be enjoyed all year round.

► **EDISFORD BRIDGE** *c1965* C122038

This was another popular area where children could paddle and swim. By 1972 a swimming pool had opened at Edisford. This scene, possibly taken in high summer after a drought, shows a low water level; but when the river was in spate, a dramatic increase in height could occur at this spot. Early bridges along the Ribble were swept away in floods, and there are many records of flood damage.

EDISFORD BRIDGE
The Camp Site c1965
C122045

At Edisford Bridge on 1 June 1985 the President of the Ramblers' Association, Mike Harding, and the Chairman of the Countryside Commission performed a ceremony to declare open the Ribble Way. The popularity of the site at this stretch of the river in 1965 is plain to see. Amusingly, the busy Tourist Board (with witches in mind) issues a challenge to 'visit Pendle if you dare!'

EDISFORD BRIDGE *1894* 34347

There was a battle on this site in 1138. Roger de Lacy, who died in 1212, gave four acres of land for the building of a leper hospital St Nicholas at Edisford, as leprosy increased after the Crusades. The bridge is of interest for its numerous masons' marks.

BRUNGERLEY FROM THE PARK *1899* 42906A

Long before the bridge was built there were stepping stones, then called 'hipping stones', at this spot. Here King Henry VI was captured after betrayal in 1464. Sitting along the river bank with a picnic was loved by the Edwardians. Even 'messing about in boats' was possible when Eli Tucker bought the old Grindleton ferry boat for 22 shillings at auction. The Tucker family had acquired 30 rowing boats before World War I, which could be hired for a shilling an hour.

▶ **CASTLE STREET**
1921 71130

Moor Lane runs alongside the castle to join Castle Street, from where the strategic position of the fortress towering high above the rooftops can be fully appreciated. Clitheroe's first purpose-built bank was erected on Castle Street in 1870 on the site of an old inn, The Brownlow Arms. The Swan and Royal Hotel is on the right, and opposite are a newsagent's signs advertising popular magazines, *The Queen* and *London Opinion*.

◀ **CASTLE STREET**
c1960 C122018

The Swan and Royal Hotel with its bait stables stands opposite Boots the chemists, and Cunningham's garage has a dominant position at the at the top of the street. The Swan's rival was the café at the Commercial Hotel, which catered for travellers and visitors passing through on a daily basis. This new café was very popular thanks to its pastry cook's expertise in making the famed Clitheroe parkin, but The Swan had greater fame in the mid 1840s, as the Royal Mail coach from Clitheroe to Hellifield ran from there. On Moor Lane, York Street, Castle Street and King Street many shops developed, built largely on the crofts of mediaeval times.

CASTLE STREET
1903 50164

Premises in the lee of the castle are burgeoning. A lady in clothes that touch the ground (left) is shopping for rugs or carpets - examples hang outside. The barber's pole next door indicates a gentleman's hairdressing shop (in earlier times a surgeon); across the street C Whiteside's cycle works (right) shows growing demand - note the tricycle (foreground left). Busborough Brothers, ironmongers (right) display oil lamps in their window (no electricity was available yet). Busborough's services were also in demand for iron and tin plate work. Barrels outside some of the shops (including Bowmans, centre) may indicate the delivery of treacle. Starkies Arms Hotel, on the extreme right, has a coat of arms above the archway - the Starkies were a local family of ancient lineage.

FRANCIS FRITH'S - CLITHEROE

CLITHEROE - THE TOWN

CASTLE STREET
1921 71133

This is the hub of the town, leading up to the castle. Motor traffic has arrived (centre left), but the horse and cart (in front of the car) are still indispensable. Immediately to the left is a greengrocer's shop with wooden orange boxes outside. Higher up from The Starkies Arms (right) is an 'authorised Ford dealer' at a garage, a sign of the times.

FRANCIS FRITH'S - CLITHEROE

▶ **FROM CASTLE STREET**
1921 71132

Emerging from King Street into the lower end of Castle Street (left) is a lady in white. This could be the heat-wave Whitsuntide of 1921. The road sweeping to the left is Church Street leading to Church Brow; the road to the right is York Street. The building on the corner with the clock is the Carnegie Library, once the site of Bailey's the corn miller's.

CLITHEROE - THE TOWN

◀ **MARKET PLACE**
c1950 C122003

We are at almost the same spot as in view 71132 (above), and we can see clearly the changes that have taken place since the early years of the century. Baileys and the drinking fountain opposite have gone, to be replaced by the Carnegie Library in 1905. York Street (right) was built as part of a new road to Chatburn. The Royal Grammar School was moved from the churchyard to York Street piece by piece. The longest serving master (47 years) was Ephraim Garthwaite.

KING STREET *c1960* C122023

It was a different scene here in 1911, when the post office (left) was situated opposite terraced houses. By the 1930s its indoor and outdoor staff numbered 32, and there were frequent deliveries and collections throughout the day. At the beginning of the century, and in coaching days, mail was collected from Bailey's the corn miller's. This scene in King Street shows (right) Aspdens, Oddies Textiles and Byrne's grocery and wines and spirits shop. A bus has appeared, the No 253 to Low Moor. King Street was changing fast, for the first motor car in Clitheroe appeared outside Number 15, where Dr A W Musson lived. It was an early Benz car. The railway station at the end of King Street opened in 1871, and the Station Hotel followed in the 1890s. The approach to the station was via Parson Lane; the station itself was on the site now occupied by Booths supermarket.

CLITHEROE - THE TOWN

MARKET PLACE *1921* 71131

This view up Castle Street from the Market Place shows The White Lion Hotel immediately on the right, with a café next door. The big lamp which replaced the drinking fountain is also serving as sign post to Sabden, 3½ miles away. The era of the motor bike with side car has arrived (centre) - this was popular for young families as a cheap way of touring further afield.

MARKET PLACE *1921* 71134

Next to Cunliffes (left) are the printing offices of the *Northern Daily Telegraph* and *Blackburn Times*, and also of the *Clitheroe Times*. The bustling town with a soaring population had much to report. Redmayne and Reed, another new concern, has appeared next to The White Lion Hotel, and a charabanc party is making for the castle. Population growth was slow in the early years of Clitheroe's history, but it rose more rapidly towards the 19th and 20th centuries.

▶ THE CASTLE
1903 50163

One famous painter, L S Lowry, visited Clitheroe many times. His paintings of the town show a great interest in its rooftops, which are well illustrated in this photograph. Rooftops echo the different periods of building. One rooftop of 1860 shows the Royal Insignia; it was the Court House, Lowergate (just out of this photograph). The free burgesses of the town held privileges expressed in 13 charters drawn up over 11 centuries.

◀ THE VIEW FROM THE CASTLE
c1950 C122005

More rooftops, a passing steam train (they were being replaced by diesel-powered locomotives at this time) and the sweep of the park express progress. The bandstand has arrived. From the bandstand in 1948 sweets were handed out to the children after sports. They were provided by former residents who had gone to live abroad but still craved news of the town.

CLITHEROE - THE TOWN

▲ **THE CASTLE GARDENS,** *The Bowling Green 1927* 80545

This is part of the castle grounds, and tournaments can be held here. Close by in 1970, on the occasion of the 800th anniversary of the first Charter, celebrations on Saturday 7 August included musical rides and spectacular events staged by the Mounted Branch of the Lancashire Constabulary - permission had been given by Captain Sir Archibald F Horden.

◄ **CHATBURN**
Crow Trees Brow c1955
C462003

Crow Trees Brow once led to Bellman Quarry, and was a leper path originally. A happy memory of the year of the 800th anniversary of Clitheroe's Norman castle was 'Betty's Bus', driven by Betty Gray of York Street at 12.45 on a Tuesday or a Thursday. Beautiful countryside and the picturesque village of Downham, where we were allowed to feed the ducks, was the reward. It was a wonderful way of seeing the westerly slopes of Pendle Hill, and a much appreciated personal service.

THE CASTLE GARDENS
The Tennis Courts 1927
80546

These are part of the improvements to the castle grounds: tennis courts, bowling green, recreation ground and gardens gay with shrubs and flowers have all added to Clitheroe's charm and growing popularity. Note the old-fashioned heavy roller (left) pulled by the groundsman to produce perfect turf. The heavier rollers had rings fitted for a horse to pull.

THE RECREATION GROUND *c1960* C122025

When the 800th anniversary celebrations of the first Charter arrived, children thronged this area. The Clitheroe Pageant presented on 31 July and 7 August 1948 acted out scenes from Clitheroe's history from 1148 to 1948 in 20 episodes. It was written by local headmasters Arthur Longshaw and Lawrence Hardy and H B Shaw, organist at the parish church. Highwaymen, monks, the Lancashire Witches and the Pilgrimage of Grace were all depicted as part of the fun.

THE MEADOWS *1927* 80533

This area of land below the castle was good for a stroll or a game - two boys are contemplating a contest of one-a-side football. A century earlier, this area was known as the Flatts. In the 1840s John Haworth, manager at Primrose Mill, lived at Flatts Row. Reports from Henthorn Farm from about 1870 read: 'gangs of men were employed to mow the meadows with long-bladed scythes. Next came the tedders with hay forks to turn the hay ready for drying in the sun'. Later still, tedding machines replaced this centuries-old method. John Winkley of King Street was a sawyer and hay rake maker. The farm carts seen in some of these photographs would be supplied by him and a neighbour of his in King Street, Theo Wilson, 'dealer in bar and hoop iron mowing and hay-making machines.'

CLITHEROE - THE TOWN

CASTLE STREET
c1950 C122006

Coleman's, selling children's and ladies' wear (right, with the two motor cars outside) was always busy. Dawson's grocer's shop was next door. Saturday shopping was easy for those without cars, for they could rely on express delivery from these two adjacent shops. Stools and chairs were provided for shoppers, and 'the customer was always right.' The Swan and Royal's reputation for politeness had been upheld, and its mews areas were becoming garages. Road signs (foreground, 'crossroads') were of necessity increasing along with the traffic.

FRANCIS FRITH'S - CLITHEROE

▶ **THE RIVER RIBBLE**
1899 42908

Tree-lined, and with lush green river banks, the River Ribble runs through pretty villages and on to Clitheroe, joining with the River Calder and the River Hodder. Flowing through picturesque countryside, it drew fishermen, bathers, boaters, picnickers galore. Over the years rules and permits had to be brought in, and a watch kept against poachers of fish and game. In the distance is Edisford bridge.

CLITHEROE - THE TOWN

▲ THE WEIR 1899 42909

Along the Ribble Way, before reaching Gisburn, the river cuts through a deep gorge, perhaps the most spectacular part of its length; but at this point we see the river harnessed. The weir, with its graceful half-circle shape, presented the chance to control and use the power of water. In the 19th century a cut was dug out from the river. The rushing water drove the engines at Low Moor spinning mill.

◄ THE VIEW FROM BOLLAND PROSPECT c1960 C122032

Here the road rises out of Clitheroe, giving a prospect of the town and castle keep. 'Bolland' is the old spelling for the now accepted one, 'Bowland'. From here the Trough of Bowland and the range of Forest of Bowland hills such as Fairsnape, Parlick Pike and Whalley Nab could be appreciated.

FRANCIS FRITH'S - CLITHEROE

FROM THE CASTLE
1927 80530

Some call the view from the castle 'a town of rooftops'. The artist L S Lowry, sketching from the castle and Church Street, found their diversity a fascination. The town's development is pictured here, and its closeness to Pendle Hill. The Whalley viaduct can be seen in the background.

▲ **THE PARISH CHURCH** *1903* 50166

There was a church on this site in 1122. In 1828 the present church of St Mary Magdalene replaced a small medieval building. The spire was added in the 1840s. It caused concern when it appeared to be twisting, but this flaw was corrected in 1969. In May 1979 a fire at the parish church caused £300,000 worth of damage, and restoration took place. Double glazing for the clerestory windows was installed, and the organ was rebuilt by George Sixsmith.

▶ **A VIEW ON THE RIBBLE** *1894*
34349

It is now possible to walk the full length of this beautiful river by the Ribble Way. Occasionally a diversion has to be made, but ramblers can trek along a route quite different from the Pennine Way. Springing in barren moorland from two becks, the Gayle and the Cam, the Ribble passes Settle, shoots Stainforth Force and calms here into a broad sparkling waterway.

CLITHEROE - THE HALLS

BOLTON HALL *1899* 42923

Home of the Pudsay family, Bolton Hall was once the hiding place of an English King, Henry VI, after his defeat at the battle of Hexham in 1464. Unfortunately, he was captured not long afterwards at Brungerley Bridge. One of the Pudsay family from Bolton Hall was remembered for a bold leap on horseback from Rainsber Scar across the River Ribble (see 42925, page 50).

▶ BOLTON HALL
1899 42925

William Pudsay, who made the desperate leap on horseback, was fleeing from the authorities, having been charged with counterfeiting coinage. Silver shillings were being made from silver mined at Rimington on his estates. William gained a pardon from Queen Elizabeth, but she claimed his silver mine. In 1950 the contents of this historic building were auctioned, and the house was demolished.

◀ STANDEN HALL
1899 42919

This became the home of Viscount Arthur Southwell and a French aristocrat, Sophia Maria Joseph, who escaped from France at the time of the French Revolution in 1792. Other members of their family also found refuge here. By 1833 this imposing house was occupied by Colonel Aspinall, who laid the foundation stone of the first Clitheroe Sunday School.

CLITHEROE - THE HALLS

▲ **WADDOW HALL** *1899* 42910

Waddow Hall is situated on the outskirts of Waddington near Brungerley Bridge; its name is derived from Wada, a Saxon chieftain. It is a Girl Guides Centre today, but it originally belonged to the lord of the manor. The story of its ghost, serving-girl Peg O'Neill, tells how she demands a drowning in the River Ribble every seven years to revenge her wronging.

◄ **DOWNHAM**
The Hall 1899 42921

The Assheton family have been linked with Downham since 1558. They purchased the lordship of the manor from the Dyneley family, and this is their Georgian-style house, which looks out towards Pendle Hill over rolling pastures. Its site was once that of a Tudor farmhouse.

▲ BASHALL EAVES
Browsholme Hall 1895 35718

For centuries this was the home of the Parker family, Bowbearers of Bowland Forest, important officials who attended the Steward's Court. Monuments to the Parker family can be found in Waddington church. The Parkers, as owners of the advowson, appointed vicars in the 19th century. Browsholme Hall was rebuilt in 1604 and improved in the 1800s. A heavy silver seal granting Puritan ministers the right to preach was kept here.

▶ WADDINGTON
The Hall 1903 50170

Over the gateway of the Old Hall is an inscription, which reads: 'I will raise up his ruins and I will build it as in the days of old.' It refers to John Waddington, who purchased the building when it had been reduced to a shabby farmhouse. In 1900 he attempted to bring back the glory of the Tempest family's dwelling when they sheltered a Lancastrian King.

WHALLEY, SAWLEY AND WADDINGTON

WHALLEY, *The Abbey 1894* 34330
Although referred to as Whalley Abbey, this building is now a conference centre owned by the diocese of Blackburn. The original abbey was founded in 1296 by a group of monks from Stanlaw, Cheshire, on land given by the lord of the manor of Clitheroe. It took nearly 200 years to complete, but now the most impressive remains are the two gateways; Whalley Abbey was desecrated under the Dissolution of the Monasteries. The ruins of the chapter house remain. Here the monks assembled daily to hear a chapter read from St Benedict's writings, founder of their order, and here original tiles have been found. The building seen in this photograph was once the manor house of the Assheton family before they moved to Downham; it was built from stone taken from the original Whalley Abbey.

FRANCIS FRITH'S - CLITHEROE

WHALLEY
Accrington Road 1914
67505

On the left, by the telegraph pole, tea rooms offer refreshments and dancing. The sett-paved road leads towards Accrington, once a part of Whalley parish. The monks of Whalley Abbey brought wealth. Stone from the abbey is to be found all over the area. Founded in 1296, this Cistercian abbey had five stages in building - the first stone was laid on St Barnabas Day, 12 June. Adam de Huddleton gave a quarry, and when two more became available, Abbot Robert's church was built. Abbot Paslew oversaw the building of the abbot's lodging and the north-east gateway. A Whalley printer bought some of the remains of the ruined abbey in 1836. The site, reconstructed in Gothic style, is well-tended today and draws hundreds of visitors.

▼ WHALLEY, *The Church 1895* 35705

The abbey church was dismantled after the hanging of Abbot Paslew. This is the third parish church, St Mary's; the first was here by 1206. Two stone coffins and a number of 13th-century gravestones (with the date February 30 on one of them) intrigue today's visitors, as do three crosses of an even earlier date, possibly of Celtic origin.

▶ WHALLEY
The Viaduct from the Nab 1901
47060

Built in the 1840s to serve the new railway age, Whalley Viaduct, bridging the valley and the River Calder, has 49 arches and is over 2000 feet long. Part of the viaduct runs along Broad Lane. Clay was dug out from the railway embankment to make the bricks for the arches. Bricklayers placed the bricks in wagons, and after firing these bricks were drawn up in wheelbarrows. The first sod of the railway line was cut on 30 December 1846 by Lord Ribblesdale. 'Puffing Billy' chugged down the line for the first time on 20 June 1850; the first stationmaster was Mr Wiggin Blackband. Clitheroe and Whalley residents were wary of the new invention, some refusing ever to use it.

WHALLEY, SAWLEY AND WADDINGTON

◀ **WHALLEY**
1921 71123

The parish of Whalley was at one time extensive, stretching beyond Burnley. A Roman road marks one boundary. The parish church of St Mary (in the distance, centre) is famous for its 15th-century choir stalls transferred from Whalley Abbey. This popular tourist area now has shops, cafés, inns and a modern library, and is a favoured commuter town.

▶ **WHALLEY**
King Street 1899 42927

This early view of King Street shows little development, although an attempt at advertising can be seen by the wall at the end of the row of houses, which is plastered with posters. Colman's mustard and Zebrite to polish black fire ovens were commonly in use, and so was Bird's custard and starch to help the busy housewife. Mr Mahlon Chilion Robinson had a wheelwright's shop in Queen Street at the time of this photograph. He built one of the flat-bottomed ferry boats for Hacking ferry in 1920, watched by daughter Mary Standen of King Street. Mary recalled: 'You had to make a loud noise to attract the ferryman when you wanted to get across.'

WHALLEY
King Street
1906 54206

Georgian houses still grace King Street, where Mrs Day was a confectioner and the grocer M Parker ran refreshment rooms (right). Three of the inns date back to c1700. The 18th-century Whalley Arms became The Hog's Head. The Swan was the chief coaching inn, where you could catch a 'flyer' for Manchester; fares to Manchester in the 19th century were 14 shillings inside the stage coach, and 10 shillings outside. Mrs Pollard's Fancy Depository (left) stood opposite The De Lacy Arms Hotel, run by landlord E E Pollard. Most streets were paved with stone setts from Accrington.

▶ **WHALLEY**
The Abbey, the Moat Bridge 1895
35710

What once was a most common defensive device in the 13th century has long been dry, but this much-photographed corner breathes 'ancient of days'. Any monk who had broken vows was flogged In the chapter house. Over the west gate a grammar school was founded in 1547 by Edward VI. Wandering the well-kept ruins, the visitor can piece together the layout of what once was a magnificent monastery.

▼ **SAWLEY**
The Village 1921 71144

Sawley is best known for Sawley Abbey, and in later years, when motor cars appeared, for dangerous Sawley Brow. Once in the West Riding of Yorkshire, it is now in Lancashire. William de Percy founded Sawley Abbey in 1146, but it was dissolved under Henry VIII's ruling. Much of the stone was used in village buildings and walls. The Spread Eagle Hotel across from the ruins accommodates travellers along the Ribble Way.

▶ **SAWLEY**
The Old Gateways 1894 34356

Sawley's name is derived from Salley or Sallei, meaning an area of willow trees. In 1146 Sawley Abbey was founded by William de Percy. The Cistercian monks favoured the site, as there was a good supply of fish in the river. As at Whalley, much stone was carried away after the Dissolution, but these gateways remain and are maintained as a commanding approach. The monks of Sawley used Monk Gate, a path at the foot of Pendle Hill.

◀ **WADDINGTON**
The Village 1903
50171

This view is very different today. The weavers' cottages of stone and slate with stone-silled 16-paned windows featuring delicate glazing bars, the old lamps and a smithy have passed into history. A hundred years ago the village was self-supporting, with farmers, craftsmen and a cotton-spinning mill.

◀ **WADDINGTON**
The Village c1965
W523029

This village once staged bull-baiting in its square, and it had a blacksmith and a wheelwright's shop; it has now became a peaceful haven for the retired and commuters proud of its long history. The Higher Buck hotel (centre), a garage and a telephone box (right) and motorised traffic show that time has marched on, but Waddington brook with its rustic bridge still flows alongside.

WHALLEY, SAWLEY AND WADDINGTON

◀ **WADDINGTON**
The Village 1903 50167

Behind The Sun Inn (right) was a small industry where chairs and bobbins were made. There was also a tannery, sited well away from the cottages because of its smell. Ribble Valley archaeological finds are on display at Ribchester Museum, including the replica of a Romano-Celtic head and metal objects from the Iron Age hill fort at Portfield, Whalley.

▼ **WADDINGTON**
The Church 1903 50169

Richard Tempest, lord of the manor, was probably advised by King Henry VI about this beautiful church in Perpendicular style when he was sheltering the royal visitor in 1500. There are interesting church records. The dog whipper was paid 6 shillings until 1840 to keep dogs out of the church. Rush bearing continued into the 19th century. The parish chest containing Poor Law accounts turned up at The Sun Inn, and its contents were sent to Lancashire Record Office - unfortunately, the chest was lost. Waddington choir had annual wagonette outings, when their driver always wore a top hat.

▶ **WADDINGTON**
The Almshouses 1899
42916

The almshouses had their own chapel; they are considered to be one of the finest group of almshouses in the country. Overlooking a pleasant green, and well maintained throughout their history, they were built for 'ten poor widows'. Robert Parker's bequest now extends to 30 widows, and more cottages have been provided. Note the nursemaid with a dog and a child on a donkey.

◀ **THE HODDER RIVER**
The Lower Hodder Bridges 1894 34339

It was on this spot on 10 June 1138 that the Scottish army defeated the English at the Battle of Clitheroe. Cromwell's army is said to have crossed the river by the furthermost bridge in 1648. When the 8000 troops passed over the 'Brig of Hoder' it was essentially a pack horse bridge. The visitor may well be amazed that its fragile-looking structure still spans the river in unused splendid isolation; it can be viewed best from the solid Lower Hodder Bridge alongside. This area is known as 'paradise', 'fine fishing and scenery but too many bridges to count.'

THE VILLAGES

DOWNHAM, *The Village 1894* 34357

This ancient village is one of the most beautiful in the country; its charm has been protected by the Assheton family since 1558. These grey stone cottages built for handloom weavers date from the 18th and 19th centuries. St Leonard's Church, a Saxon foundation, stands in the field named Kirkacre. A steep street connects the cottages around the church with those at the top of the village. In 1890 James Greenwood was the miller, and Elizabeth Beesley ran the village grocer's shop.

DOWNHAM, *Pendle Hill 1921* 71191

By 1921 there was a reservoir at the foot of Pendle Hill. The hill, 7 miles long and 1837 feet high, shelters Clitheroe from the east. The villages had from time immemorial been troubled with floods in rainy seasons, but the reservoir solved this problem, and answered the demands for water in a growing district. Downham village, steeped in history because of its position, is one of the prettiest and least spoiled villages in Lancashire; but much of its lure can be attributed to the notorious Lancashire witches, still said to haunt the area. The novelist Harrison Ainsworth exploited the story, and many others have followed, whilst television and radio have picked up the theme in later years. The so-called witches, a group of desperately poor and ignorant families, lived on the slopes of Pendle. Having been suspected of casting spells and holding covens, they were tried at Lancaster Castle; ten of them were executed in August 1612, 'Demdike', 'Old Chattox' and Alice Nutter amongst them.

THE VILLAGES

DOWNHAM
Cottages near the Church 1921 71185

The church of St Leonard has a tower of 15th-century origin, but a church has been on the same site since the 13th century. Work on the village was undertaken in 1910 when the post office was provided and the church as we see it today was built. The oldest inhabitant at the time of this photograph was William Parkinson of Chestnut Row, aged 90. He played the cello, and had been a hand loom weaver.

DOWNHAM, *The Village 1921* 71189

This pastoral scene posed by the photographer is charming; it shows the steep village street leading to the cottages grouped around the stocks, church and inn. The two men with the horse are not far from the brook which runs through Downham - it is the haunt of white ducks and mallard. On 24 and 25 May 1986, twelve Morris teams, along with the Clitheroe Morris Men, danced at Downham to mark the 800th anniversary of Clitheroe Castle.

SABDEN
The Wesleyan Church and Wesley Street c1960 S691011

Lying in a beautiful valley between the Ribble and Calder rivers, Sabden also has the backdrop of Pendle Hill to remind us of its association with the Pendle Witches and their covens - Demdike Crafts, a shop in Sabden, sells 'witch' souvenirs. The Wesleyan church was a participant in the Whitsuntide Walking days. A feature of the processions was hymn singing by choirs who were very well-trained and renowned in the districts of Pendle and Whalley. The Clitheroe Glee Singers were famous in my grandparents' time.

BARLEY
The Village and Pendle Hill c1960 B892008

Barley is yet another small, picturesque village clustered low on Pendle Hill. The 1,837-foot hill dominates Barley and a wide area of farmland. From here walkers can reach the site of the beacon which warned of Scottish raiders and was ignited at the time of the Spanish Armada. Pendle Inn at the centre of Barley is a favourite meeting place for walkers and cyclists, and Barley also has a picnic site with a close view of Pendle Hill.

THE VILLAGES

▲ **STONYHURST,** *The College 1899* 43489

For 400 years, until the family line died out, the influential Shireburnes lived at Stonyhurst. Each generation made changes. The building with its towers and cupolas was designed by Sir Nicholas Shireburne, but he lost his son and heir and on his death in 1717 the estate passed to his daughter. Another descendant, Thomas Weld, leased the building to a Jesuit teaching order; it became a famous Roman Catholic public school, attended by such notables as Charles Laughton, the actor. Gerard Manley Hopkins, the poet, studied for the Jesuit priesthood here. It was the first public building to be lit by gas.

◄ **STONYHURST**
The Meteorological Department 1899
43493

The Jesuit owners of the college had the Herculean task of transforming a historical building into a teaching establishment. This observatory was available for use by 1912 and as the repair and reconstruction programme progressed, classrooms, dormitories, museum and library were added. The telescope, used by thousands of students, was installed in 1893 and known as the Perry Memorial to commemorate a famous Jesuit astronomer, father Stephen Perry. Between 1832 and 1835 St Peter's Church was built. The refectory is part of the Elizabethan house of Sir Richard Shireburne, who provided the almshouses near Ribchester and the village school at Hurst Green. The almshouses, originally built at Kemple End in 1706, were dismantled and re-assembled for use by workers at Stonyhurst College.

▲ HURST GREEN
The Cross c1950 H445011

From early days this village attracted tourists because of its proximity to Stonyhurst. It had two ferries across the river: Hacking Boat near Winckley Hall farm, and the other at Trough House. The latter stopped when the bridge at Dinckley was built. The Hurst Green Brass Band played for 100 years, but this too has ended, sad to say. The Eagle and Child Inn (centre) and the café (right) serving Pyper's ices near the Cross were very busy in summer.

▶ HURST GREEN
The Village c1955 H445036

On the right is a typical old Ribble Valley inn, The Bayley Arms - note its stone quoins. Hand-loom weaving in its heyday caused three bobbin mills to be built, one given over now to plastics. The village blacksmith, Joe Walmsley, was one of the local characters, and Hurst Green also rejoiced in a village policeman for all of 130 years.

THE VILLAGES

WEST BRADFORD, *The Village 1921* 71150

James Leeming's Millstone Inn is on the right, with its unusual inn sign of three millstones pictorially displayed on the wall. Cobbled yards, old stone cottages and the inn with its original windows combine to give an impression of a time warp. The sound of the bells of Pendle country float overhead, reminding one of a centuries-old rhyme and warning to bell ringers:-

'Whoever a bell doth overthrowe
Shall paye two groate before he go.
And he that ringed with his hatte on
Shalle paye two groate and then be gone
And he that ring with spur on heele
Likewise that penalty shall feele
And he that does an oathe swear
For that shall paye to quartes of beare.'

GREAT MITTON
The Church from the River Ribble 1921 71154

All Hallows Church (right) was built in Edward III's reign, and contains a leper squint and the magnificent Shireburne Chapel. The two hamlets of Little Mitton and Great Mitton are separated by the river, which makes a beautiful setting. Some cottages had a 'witch post' to hold a crooked sixpence; this would, the villagers thought, speed the butter churning.

GREAT MITTON, *The Bridge 1921* 71155

This is one of the fine strong stone bridges spanning the River Ribble. The ferry boat at Hacking End once took people across for one penny, a long-established custom, so old that it is not known when it began; but in the 1930s the practice finished.

THE VILLAGES

▲ **GREAT MITTON**
The Village 1899 43494

A group of villagers in their best clothes, along with the maid from the inn, are caught by the photographer. It was a sleepy day in 1899 in a farming community. Derived from 'Mythe', a Saxon name, Mitton has a famous old rhyme linked with its history: 'Rivers Ribble, Hodder, Calder and Rain All meet together at Mitton domain.' The lovely old church contains the chancel screen from Sawley Abbey.

WISWELL, *The Village 1906* 54218

Wiswell is an old village on the western slope of Pendle Hill looking towards the Trough of Bowland. Reference is made to Wiswell in a charter of 1193. Hand-loom weaving and quarrying sandstone occupied villagers in the past, but the area is now residential. Wiswell Old Hall was the home of Abbot Paslew, and it is said that his ghost walks. After the Pilgrimage of Grace, draconian punishments were handed out: Abbot Paslew was hanged, drawn and quartered. Only 4 miles from Wiswell is the 7-acre lake created in 1885 as one of Clitheroe's reservoirs. By the mid 20th century it had become redundant, and was bought by Robert J Mountford-Aram to turn into the Whalley Abbey Reservoir trout fishery. He stocked it with rainbow trout, and granted permits for recreational fishing in 1977.

WHITEWELL, *The Hotel 1921* 71247

The Whitewell Hotel in the Hodder Valley has long been famed for its hospitality and proximity to good fishing. Another view of brooding Pendle Hill can be had from Whitewell. The wooded area along the river moving towards the Trough of Bowland is said to be reminiscent of Switzerland.

THE VILLAGES

WHITEWELL
1921 71260

The hotel at Whitewell was then the last licensed premises before the Trough of Bowland. Here the visitors could also cross the river Hodder by the Spring Bridge and watch trout in the clear waters. Baked trout was a speciality at Whitewell Hotel.

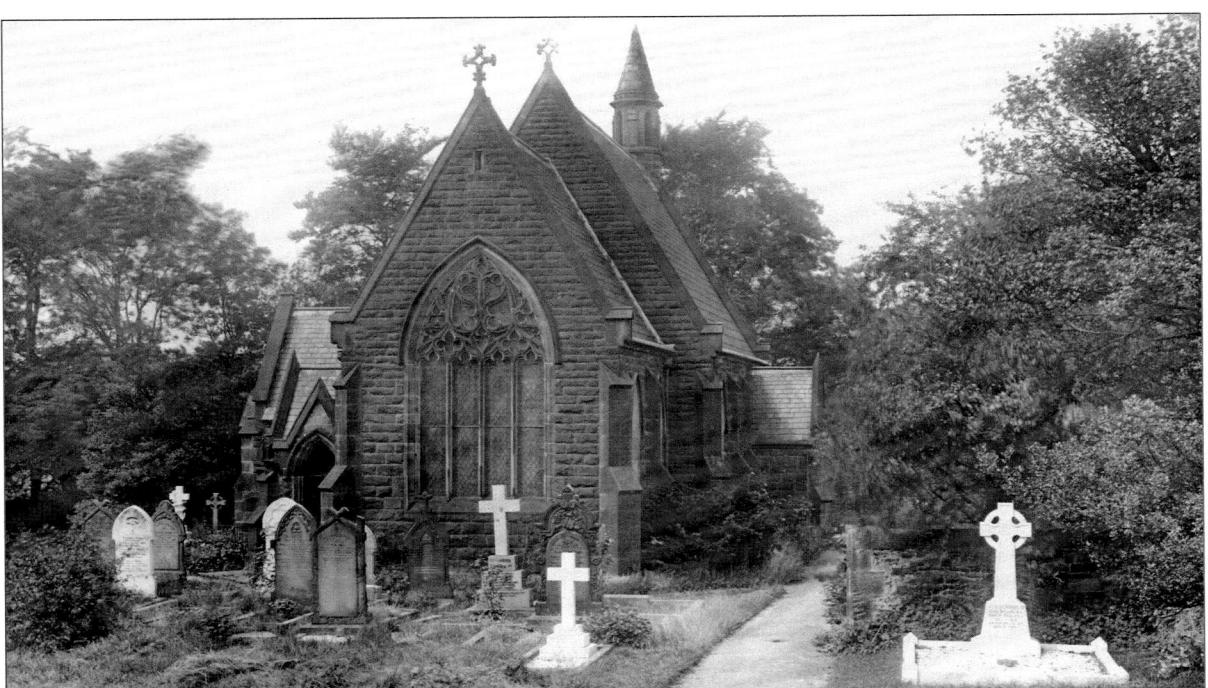

PENDLETON, *The Church 1921* 71163

A philanthropic lady, Mrs Blegborough, had the church of All Saints built in 1846, and later paid for the vicarage to be erected. A village with long history (a bronze age urn found in Pendleton is now in Clitheroe museum), Pendleton was mentioned in William the Conqueror's *Domesday Book*. For several generations a branch of the de Hoghton family occupied Pendleton Hall.

PENDLETON
The Village 1921 71165

This view shows the stream that runs through this ancient village of stone houses. In Old Post Office Row lived 'Little Ellen', a 19th-century teacher's daughter; she kept the post office and never left the village. A tiny lady, she was 89 when she died. A long-established Pendle family, the Nutters, took over the post office, which is now situated in another part of the village.

WORSTON, 1921 71162

This panoramic scene is typical of the Clitheroe villages: houses shelter in the lee of hills and trees, with open country beyond. Primroses, sloes, wood sorrel, wood anemones, shepherd's purse, gorse, celandine and butterbur are just a few of the species to be found at different seasons. Ramblers, cyclists, geologists and naturalists find Worston and its neighbouring villages of interest all year round. For those following the Witch Country trail, Worston's Crow Cottage had a circular window designed, according to legend, for a witch to fly through on her broomstick. A relic from bull-baiting days is still in the village: a strong iron ring in the ground to which the bull was tethered. Worston Old Hall had three stone shields, thought to have come from either Sawley or Whalley Abbey.

THE VILLAGES

WORSTON
The Village 1894 34359

Clitheroe is surrounded by lovely villages. Like Chatburn, Worston is part of the Honour of Clitheroe. Around the date of this photograph, James Badger was innkeeper of the Calf's Head. Historical records show that in the 16th century Worston was flooded to such an extent that the furniture floated out of the cottages. This was due to a freak torrent of water bursting out of Pendle Hill from a subterranean area. In the 13th century the de Lacy family imposed some quaint rents on tenants, such as '2 collars for hounds and a pair of gloves payable on the feast of St Oswald.'

NEWCHURCH-IN-PENDLE, *The Village c1960* N191010
A character in this 18th-century village was Nanny Maud, who lived at the top end of the village; from here she extracted a one penny toll whenever a carrier's cart passed her house. Known then as a 'wise woman' (not a witch), she would no doubt be called street-wise three centuries later!

THE VILLAGES

GRINDLETON
The Village 1921 71175

In the village centre stand two inns, The Duke of York and The Buck, where the 'Hen Pecked Club' used to gather for a hearty meal after a procession led by the brass band. In Slater's Directory of 1900, 52 farmers are listed. Sulphur and lime springs benefited visitors to the Hydro Hotel, and some villagers recall how weavers shrank their tweed cloth at Wortwell's Well, but handloom weaving became a thing of the past. Narrow ginnels linked Back Lane with Main Street, where the post office stood in 1921. Grindleton is another Ribble Valley village which has been subjected to boundary changes and the conversion of barns, but it remains a charming backwater, quietly famous for damsons and damson gin. It once had a jam factory. H Smalley's grocer and general dealer's shop (left) would be handy for villagers.

GRINDLETON
The Village and the Post Office 1921 71173

The steep village street passes the post office (left), which was equipped with a public telephone, a rarity in 1921. Behind the village, in whose centre roads to Slaidburn and Sawley connect, are the high moorlands. There are almshouses on the Sawley road, which were built in 1860. William Bank was the miller at Grindleton in 1900.

GRINDLETON
The Bridge and the River Ribble 1921 71172

The gradients of the valley of the River Ribble have become more gentle as it broadens and lush pastures are reached. The Grindleton Bridge is one point from which one can strike off for the Ribble Way. Just a few miles on, walkers can take Cold Park wood and Steep Wood in their stride. This fine photograph features 'Old Pendle's' allure.

RIMINGTON
Main Street c1955 R273004

Boundary changes in the 20th century have caused this village to be in Yorkshire, then in Lancashire, and then back again in Yorkshire. The old sawmill, barns and some farmhouses have been converted into dwellings in a village where lead mining and farming once employed the majority. Francis Duckworth, composer of the well-known hymn *Rimington*, was born next door to the Methodist chapel. He was brought up by parents who kept a shop at nearby Stopper Lane; the whole family were strict Methodists.

THE VILLAGES

BASHALL EAVES, *The Village c1955*
B742001

Dating from Saxon times, throughout its long history the village's name changes have included 'Bakesalt', 'Bascleef' and 'Backhalgh'. It has a lovely setting on the banks of the river Hodder, with Bashall Brook, a tributary of the River Ribble, spanning its eastern boundary. A historic coaching inn, the Red Pump, is known to have stood here in the early 1700s; it was occasionally visited by press gangs forcing men and boys into serving on board ship.

BASHALL EAVES *The Hall Gates c1955*
B742012

These gates lead to 15th-century Bashall Hall, the home of the Talbot family, who kept a private army and betrayed King Henry VI. For this treachery King Edward IV rewarded Thomas Talbot with £100 and a pension. A half-timbered building, still in a good condition, stands behind Bashall Hall; this was where Thomas Talbot's retainers and soldiers lived.

CHATBURN
The Tollhouse c1955
C462004

The large sign on what was once a toll house, judging by its shape and position on the road junction, points to Gisburn, a neighbouring village. Some newer property has been built on the right, but the lamp is a genuine piece of old street furniture, and some solid stone walls continue to endure. The toll house, built in 1826, served in modern times as Hudson's ice cream shop. Examples of toll charges were: 'Horse 3 pence, Score of Oxen 1s 3d, Wagon with 6 horses 6 shillings, coach drawn by 6 horses 6 shillings.'

CHATBURN, *The Village 1921* 71178
On the right is The Brown Cow Inn, supplied by the Blackburn Brewery Company, who also supplied the inn lower down. Outside it there appears to be a group of men eyeing with interest a three-wheeled car. It was possibly a Morgan, which was then a novelty. The Black Bull, built in 1855, was a popular meeting place, and one to repair to if and when your Morgan turned over. Having only three wheels it could suddenly do this!

INDEX

Barley 70
Bashall Eaves 52, 84-85
Bolton Hall 49, 50-51
Brungerley Bridge 24-25
Brungerley from the Park 27
Castle 15, 16, 38-39, 46-47
Castle Entrance 17, 22
Castle Gardens 39-40
Castle Grounds 18
Castle House 16
Castle Street 28-29, 30-31, 32-33, 34-35, 42-43
Chatburn 12, 39, 86
Church Street 23
Downham 10, 51, 66-67, 68, 69
Edisford Bridge 25, 26
Great Mitton 74, 75
Grindleton 80-81, 82-83, 84
Hodder River 64-65
Hurst Green 72
King Street 36
Market Place 22-23, 34-35, 37
Meadows 41
Newchurch-in-Pendle 79
Parish Church 48
Pendleton 77, 78
Recreation Ground 40
Rimington 84
River Ribble 44
Sabden 70-71
Sawley 60-61
Standen Hall 50
Stonyhurst 71
View from Bolland Prospect 44-45
View from the Castle 19, 20-21, 38
View on the Ribble 48
Waddington 52, 61, 62-63, 64-65
Waddow Hall 51
Weir 45
West Bradford 73
Whalley 13, 53, 54-55, 56-57, 58-59, 60
Whitewell 76-77
Wiswell 76
Worston 78, 79

NAMES OF SUBSCRIBERS

The following people have kindly supported this book by subscribing to copies before publication

The Adcroft Family
In Memory of Alan Ainsworth, Sabden, Clitheroe
Alison & Chris, Long Marton, Cumbria
To Mike with love from Alexander Anders & Dorte 22 May 2004
Sandra & Steve Ashcroft
Mr Eric Badger
John Bailey
William & Jean Bailey
The Baldwin Family, Bashall Eaves
In Memory of James Baxter, Chadwick
Bert Bessant
Mr & Mrs K Bolton
Gifted by the Bowker Family of Clitheroe
In Memory of Mrs Margaret Patterson Bowker of Clitheroe
In Memory of John W. B. Boyce, Clitheroe
Dan Bradbury
In celebration of the Buckley / Hill Wedding 01/12/03
Mr A. W. Burn & Mrs D Burn, Clitheroe
Mr George & Mrs Nancy Campbell
Mr A. D. & Mrs. J. E. Caunce and Family
In memory of the Clarke Family of Close Nook Farm, Rishton
Olwyn & Graham Claydon, Clitheroe
Allan Cook
William Barry Cook
Barbara & Harold Cooper
Mrs Beryl Cottam, Clitheroe
The Cowburn Family, Clitheroe
Cowperthwaite Family, Clitheroe & Davies Family, Rishton
Mr & Mrs N. Davey, Bolton-By-Bowland
Mr J. S. & Mrs J. Dean, Low Moor, Clitheroe
Marlene Dickens, Whalley
Violet Donnelly and Family from Jean & Brian
Alan & Glynis D. Duckworth
Graham Dudley, West Bradford

The Dugdale Family, West Bradford
J. C. Dugdale, Lytham St Annes
F. R. & M. M. Eccles, Hurst Green
Mr A. T. Elliott & Miss C. I. R. Kilner, Clitheroe
Anthony Ellis
Mr. F. & Mrs. J. H. Ellison
To my wife Sheila Ennis
A. G. Farthing
In Memory of Jimmy Fell of Whalley
John & Carole Field, Clitheroe
In memory of William Fishwick from Padiham
Mrs Anne M. Fletcher, Sabden, Clitheroe
Gail & Matthew from Jean & Brian
The Gardner Family, Highmoor Park, Clitheroe
Tony Garner, Clitheroe
In Memory of Walter Garner of Clitheroe
Walter & Maureen Garner
Trevor & Maureen Gate, Clitheroe
The Giles Family, Clitheroe
Keith & Barbara Goldsmith, Clitheroe
Ralph & Dorothy Goldsmith, Clitheroe
Mrs Linda Goodbier
John & Sally Goodman retired to Clitheroe February 2004
Meg Gordon & Giles Lawson, Clitheroe
Florence Grundy, Vancouver (ex Clitheronian)
Mr. P. & Mrs. J. R. Guy
Mr K. W. Hall & Mrs M Hall, Downham
Marlene Hardy, Baxenden
Keith, Heather, Zoe & Mark Hargreaves of Clitheroe
Derek & Sandra Hargreaves, Chatburn In Memory of Mark
Mike & Gill Haworth, Clitheroe
Mr T. O. & Mrs M. T. Haworth, Whalley
Ian J. Haythornthwaite
John D. Heaton, Msc, Preston and Hants
The Higson Family, Clitheroe
In Memory of Michael J. Holmes, Langho
Mr I. M. & Mrs N. A. Hothersall, Clitheroe

Bruce & Carole Houlker
Mr M. & Mrs. L. E. Houlker & Family, Clitheroe
Suzanne L. Houlker, Clitheroe
Inner Lodge, Holden, Bolton by Bowland
In Memory of H. A. Jackson, Chatburn
In Memory of Tracey Jackson, Barrow, Clitheroe
Stanley Jervis, Clitheroe
With Best Regards Johnson Matthey Catalysts, Clitheroe
The Johnston Family, Clitheroe
The Jones Family, Clitheroe
The Jones Family, Downham
The Kemp Family
Kevin & Fiona Knight, Low Moor
Trevor Knowles
The Lambert Family, Rimington
The Lancaster Family, Clitheroe
Stephen. L. Laycock, Bsc, Barnoldswick
Derek & Valerie Leigh, Clitheroe
All descendants of George Life of Copgrove, Wry
Mr E. B. Lofthouse, Clitheroe
Amedeo & Judith Loi, Clitheroe
Mr W. & M. Lord & Family
Lisa H. N. Mantle
Margaret & Steve from Jean & Brian
The McNab Family, Barrow, Clitheroe
To Michael love Mum
David Moon
Claire Mulligan & Glyn Williams, Barrow
J. A. Myerscough, West Bradford, Clitheroe
Mrs M. A. Parker, Gt Harwood
Samuel John Parker, Clitheroe
In Memory of Richard Parkington, Clitheroe
Derek, Lisa, Natasha & Dominic Parrott, Clitheroe
Mr S. B. Payne & Mrs. A. Payne & Ellis, Blackburn
The Melville Perry Family, Stonyhurst
M. E. Price, In Memory of Mr & Mrs Robert Tomlinson, Clitheroe
The Pye Family, Clitheroe
In memory of the Rawcliffe & Hatton Families, Hurst Green
Ian Rayner, Clitheroe

Stuart Read, Rising Bridge
J & C Roberts, Clitheroe
Miss Jean Rodger
In Memory of Eddie Rothwell
Miles J. E. Rushton
John & Helen Rushton
The Sharp Family, Clitheroe
P Shepherd
Mr C. G. Skellorn & Mrs L. Skellorn, Clitheroe
In Memory of William & Mary Slinger, Clitheroe
Florence Smithies
Mr. K. Stewart-Hargreaves, Nottingham
Colin Taylor
Mr. L. & Mrs M. J. Taylor
The Taylor Family, Clitheroe
John & Sheila Temme
The Thompson Family, Clitheroe
The Thornber Family, Clitheroe
The Thorton - Bryar Family
Mrs M. Veronica Threlfall
Mr M. T. & Mrs M. Turnbull
Kay Valovin
The Wakeling Family, Clitheroe
Mr & Mrs Bob Wallbank and Kathleen
In Memory of Charlie Walmsley, Clitheroe 1910-2000
Mr & Mrs A. Warrington & Family
V. Waterhouse & P. J. Waterhouse, Clitheroe
E. Waterworth, son of Robert Waterworth
W. R. Weaver, Billington
Malcolm D. Westwood, Dunsop Bridge
G & L Wharton, Bashall Eaves, Clitheroe
Mr L. F. & Mrs. P. A. White, Sabden
The Wigan Family, Rimington
Mr I. & Mrs B. Wilkinson & Family, Simonstone
The Williamson Family, Clitheroe
Rodney & Ann Wilson and Family, Clitheroe
Mr G. H. & Mrs K. Wilson
Adrian Wintle & Alice Wintle, Clitheroe
The Woods Family, Clitheroe
Peter R. Worden, Blackburn
Mr G E & Mrs H Wrathall
In Memory of G. H. Yates, Clitheroe
Alan Yearing, Mayor of Clitheroe 1999-2001

FRITH PRODUCTS & SERVICES

Francis Frith would doubtless be pleased to know that the pioneering publishing venture he started in 1860 still continues today. Over a hundred and forty years later, The Francis Frith Collection continues in the same innovative tradition and is now one of the foremost publishers of vintage photographs in the world. Some of the current activities include:

INTERIOR DECORATION

Today Frith's photographs can be seen framed and as giant wall murals in thousands of pubs, restaurants, hotels, banks, retail stores and other public buildings throughout the country. In every case they enhance the unique local atmosphere of the places they depict and provide reminders of gentler days in an increasingly busy and frenetic world.

PRODUCT PROMOTIONS

Frith products are used by many major companies to promote the sales of their own products or to reinforce their own history and heritage. Frith promotions have been used by Hovis bread, Courage beers, Scots Porage Oats, Colman's mustard, Cadbury's foods, Mellow Birds coffee, Dunhill pipe tobacco, Guinness, and Bulmer's Cider.

GENEALOGY AND FAMILY HISTORY

As the interest in family history and roots grows world-wide, more and more people are turning to Frith's photographs of Great Britain for images of the towns, villages and streets where their ancestors lived; and, of course, photographs of the churches and chapels where their ancestors were christened, married and buried are an essential part of every genealogy tree and family album.

FRITH PRODUCTS

All Frith photographs are available Framed or just as Mounted Prints and unmounted versions. These may be ordered from the address below. Other products available are - Calendars, Jigsaws, Canvas Prints, Mugs, Tea Towels, Tableware and local and prestige books.

THE INTERNET

Over several hundred thousand Frith photographs can be viewed and purchased on the internet through the Frith websites!

For more detailed information on Frith products, look at www.francisfrith.com

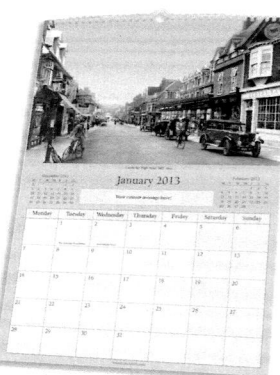

See the complete list of Frith Books at: www.francisfrith.com
This web site is regularly updated with the latest list of publications from The Francis Frith Collection. If you wish to buy books relating to another part of the country that your local bookshop does not stock, you may purchase on-line.

For further information, trade, or author enquiries please contact us at the address below:
The Francis Frith Collection, Unit 19 Kingsmead Business Park, Gillingham, Dorset SP8 5FB.
Tel: +44 (0)1722 716 376   Email: sales@francisfrith.co.uk

See Frith products on the internet at www.francisfrith.com

FREE PRINT OF YOUR CHOICE
CHOOSE A PHOTOGRAPH FROM THIS BOOK
+ POSTAGE

Mounted Print
Overall size 14 x 11 inches (355 x 280mm)

TO RECEIVE YOUR FREE PRINT

Choose any Frith photograph in this book

Simply complete the Voucher opposite and return it with your payment (to cover postage and handling) and we will print the photograph of your choice in SEPIA (size 11 x 8 inches) and supply it in a cream mount ready to frame (overall size 14 x 11 inches).

Order additional Mounted Prints at HALF PRICE - £19.00 each (normally £38.00)

If you would like to order more Frith prints from this book, possibly as gifts for friends and family, you can buy them at half price (with no additional postage costs).

Have your Mounted Prints framed

For an extra £20.00 per print you can have your mounted print(s) framed in an elegant polished wood and gilt moulding, overall size 16 x 13 inches (no additional postage required).

IMPORTANT!

❶ Please note: aerial photographs and photographs with a reference number starting with a "Z" are not Frith photographs and cannot be supplied under this offer.

❷ Offer valid for delivery to one UK address only.

❸ These special prices are only available if you use this form to order. You must use the ORIGINAL VOUCHER on this page (no copies permitted). We can only despatch to one UK address.

❹ This offer cannot be combined with any other offer.

As a customer your name & address will be stored by Frith but not sold or rented to third parties. Your data will be used for the purpose of this promotion only.

Send completed Voucher form to:
**The Francis Frith Collection,
1 Chilmark Estate House, Chilmark,
Salisbury, Wiltshire SP3 5DU**

Voucher for **FREE** and Reduced Price Frith Prints

Please do not photocopy this voucher. Only the original is valid, so please fill it in, cut it out and return it to us with your order.

Picture ref no	Page no	Qty	Mounted @ £19.00	Framed + £20.00	Total Cost £
		1	Free of charge*	£	£
			£19.00	£	£
			£19.00	£	£
			£19.00	£	£
			£19.00	£	£
			£19.00	£	£
			* Post & handling		£3.80
			Total Order Cost		£

*Please allow 28 days for delivery.
Offer available to one UK address only*

Title of this book ....

I enclose a cheque/postal order for £ ....
made payable to 'Heritage Resource Management Ltd'

OR please debit my Mastercard / Visa / Maestro card, details below

Card Number:

Issue No (Maestro only):   Valid from (Maestro):

Card Security Number: Expires:

Signature:

Name Mr/Mrs/Ms ....

Address ....

....

....

.... Postcode ....

Daytime Tel No ....

Email ....

Valid to 31/12/26

Free Print - see overleaf

Can you help us with information about any of the Frith photographs in this book?

We are gradually compiling an historical record for each of the photographs in the Frith archive. It is always fascinating to find out the names of the people shown in the pictures, as well as insights into the shops, buildings and other features depicted.

If you recognize anyone in the photographs in this book, or if you have information not already included in the author's caption, do let us know. We would love to hear from you, and will try to publish it in future books or articles.

An Invitation from The Francis Frith Collection to Share Your Memories

The 'Share Your Memories' feature of our website allows members of the public to add personal memories relating to the places featured in our photographs, or comment on others already added. Seeing a place from your past can rekindle forgotten or long held memories. Why not visit the website, find photographs of places you know well and add YOUR story for others to read and enjoy? We would love to hear from you!

www.francisfrith.com/memories

Our production team

Frith books are produced by a small dedicated team at offices near Salisbury. Most have worked with the Frith Collection for many years. All have in common one quality: they have a passion for the Frith Collection.

Frith Books and Gifts

We have a wide range of books and gifts available on our website utilising our photographic archive, many of which can be individually personalised.

www.francisfrith.com